Epic Graphic Novel
CRAFTS

by Jen Jones

4D™
An Augmented Reading
Crafting
Experience

CAPSTONE PRESS
a capstone imprint

Dabble Lab Books are published by Capstone Press,
1710 Roe Crest Drive
North Mankato, Minnesota 56003

www.mycapstone.com

Library of Congress Cataloging-in-Publication Data
Cataloging-in-Publication Data is available on the Library of Congress website.
ISBN 978-1-5435-0688-4 (library binding)
ISBN 978-1-5435-0692-1 (eBook PDF)

Editorial Credits
Mari Bolte, editor; Lori Bye, designer; Morgan Walters, media researcher;
Kathy McColley, production specialist

Photo Credits: All photographs by Capstone Studio/Karon Dubke except:
Shutterstock: Neti.OneLove, design element throughout, Ziablik, design element
throughout

Printed and bound in the USA.
010760S18

TABLE OF CONTENTS

GET LOST IN THE PAGES!

In the space where pictures meet words, you'll find the world of graphic novels—and you just might never want to leave. This style of visual storytelling takes many forms, from hauntingly beautiful black-and-white manga to colorful superhero stories to reimagined classics. It's an entirely different reading experience, and it's geared toward readers of all levels and interests!

So what better inspiration for DIY art than graphic novels—where stories become art? The crafts in this book pay a playful tribute to common themes and objects found in manga and graphic novels. Some of the projects call for graphic novel pages as materials, while others allow you to showcase your favorite scenes and characters. So make lots of room, because you're about to have an awesome art collection to go along with your graphic novel collection!

Download the Capstone 4D app!

- Ask an adult to search in the Apple App Store or Google Play for "Capstone 4D".
- Click Install (Android) or Get, then Install (Apple).
- Open the app.
- Scan any of the following spreads with this icon:

When you scan a spread, you'll find fun extra stuff to go with this book! You can also find these things on the web at *www.capstone4D.com* using the password: ncc.graphicnovels

CHARMED LIFE

In Italian, the phrase *Mangia* means "eat," and that's what characters do in *manga* with tasty Japanese treats! This fun clay charm pays tribute to *onigiri* rice balls—just one of the many delish foods found in manga.

What You'll Need:

white polymer clay
colored pencil
black polymer clay
plastic blade tool
old toothbrush
small eye pin

toothpick or ball
stylus
black and pink
acrylic paint
necklace chain

Steps:

1. Take a small amount of white polymer clay (about the size of a gumball). Roll it between your fingers for a few minutes. This will warm the clay and shape it into a smooth ball. Use your fingers to mold it into a flat triangle shape with rounded corners.

2. Use the colored pencil like a rolling pin to flatten a small ball of black clay.

3. Use the plastic blade to cut the black clay into a small rectangle.

4. Add some texture by patting the black clay with a toothbrush. This will make the black clay look like dried seaweed. Then wrap the black clay around the white triangle.

5. Insert the small eye pin into the top of the white clay triangle.

6. With an adult's help, bake the polymer clay piece according to package instructions.

7. Once the *onigiri* has cooled, use the toothpick to paint on black eyes and a smile. Dot on pink circles for cheeks. Let the paint dry completely.

8. Thread the necklace chain through the pinhole to wear your new creation!

NOW TRY THIS!

To give the ball a more "rice"-like texture, use a toothpick to poke tiny dents all over the surface before baking.

KOKESHI
CUTIES

These traditional handmade Japanese dolls are known for their delicate beauty. They're popular across the anime and manga art world. Capture the Kokeshi essence with these easy-to-make bookends!

What You'll Need:

two empty, clean plastic
    bear-shaped honey bottles
funnel
sand
masking tape
red spray paint
black paper
small flower stickers
hot glue and hot glue gun
black and pink acrylic paint
fine detail paintbrush

Steps:

1. Remove the lid from one plastic bottle. Use a funnel to fill the bottle with sand. Re-attach cap when finished.

2. Cover the bear's face with tape.

3. Once the face is protected, ask an adult to spray paint the bear's body. You may want to do this step outside to avoid making a mess! Let the paint dry. Then remove the tape.

4. Use black paper to create a hairdo framing the bear's face. Decorate the hair with flower stickers. Use hot glue to attach the hair.

5. Some honey bears will already have eyes and noses, while others will be blank. For bottles without faces, use black paint to create the eyes. Either way, you will want to paint a tiny pink mouth and small pink dots on the cheeks. Let dry.

6. To add clothing details, use the black paint to make a curved diagonal line. It should stretch from the right side of the neck all the way down to the bottom left side. Paint another line from the left side of the neck to meet the first line you created. This will create the illusion of a robe.

7. Add flower stickers to the kimono in the pattern of your choice.

8. Repeat steps 1 through 7 on the second bottle. Your Kokeshi Cutie bookends are ready to stand up to your manga collection!

9

MAKE YOUR
MARK

The *kasa-obake* is a mythical ghost from Japanese folklore that's sometimes seen in manga. It commonly takes the form of an umbrella that springs to life once it turns 100 years old. And thanks to this fun bookmark craft, you can bring this popular one-eyed character to life too.

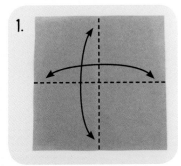

What You'll Need:

origami paper
glue stick
craft knife
large googly eye

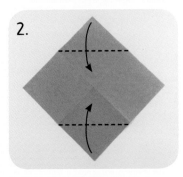

Steps:

1. Valley fold the paper in half in both directions and unfold.

2. Rotate the paper 45 degrees. Valley fold the top and bottom points to the center crease.

3. Valley fold in half.

4. Valley fold the left point along the center crease.

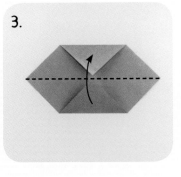

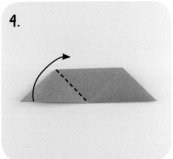

NOW TRY THIS!

Valley folds are creases made as the top surface of the paper is folded against itself.

TURN THE PAGE

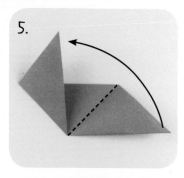

5.

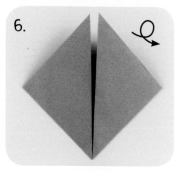

6.

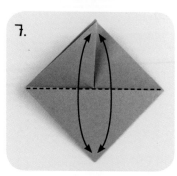

7.

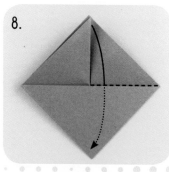

8.

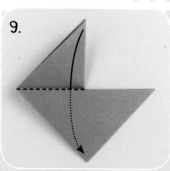

9.

10.

5. Repeat step 4 on the right side.

6. Turn the paper over.

7. Valley fold both triangle points down and unfold.

8. Tuck the top right point into the front pocket.

9. Repeat step 8 on the left side.

10. Decorate the bottom edge of the *kasa-obake* with washi tape.

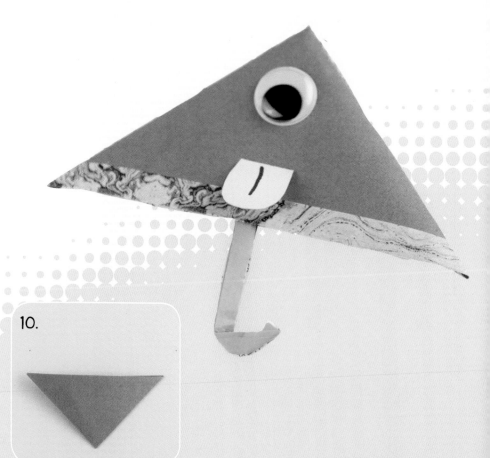

11. To make the *kasa-obake's* leg, trim a piece of origami paper to 1 ½-by-3 inches (3.8-by-7.6 centimeters). Fold a thin strip along one of the long edges. Make the strip as thin as possible.

12. Continue folding the paper's edge, creasing firmly after each fold.

13. When you reach the last ½ inch (1.3 cm), cover the inside of the paper with the glue stick. Then continue folding until you reach the end of the paper.

14. Bend the paper into a wide V shape. Glue one end inside the bookmark. Bend the other end a little, to give your *kasa-obake* a foot.

15. Have an adult help you cut a slit in the top layer of the bookmark. Then cut a small piece of origami paper to make a tongue shape. Glue it so it's coming out of the slit.

16. Glue a googly eye to the umbrella.

11.

14.

15.

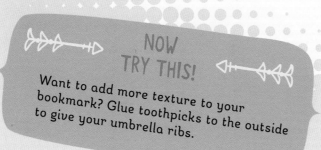

NOW
TRY THIS!

Want to add more texture to your bookmark? Glue toothpicks to the outside to give your umbrella ribs.

HOUSE OF
CARDS

Want to stack the deck for creating a one-of-a-kind craft?
This awesome card castle project is sure to deliver.

What You'll Need:

old graphic novel(s)
9 playing cards
pencil
scissors
spray adhesive
hot glue and hot glue gun

To Make the Cards:

1. Choose and tear out nine pictures from the books.

2. Grab a playing card and pencil. Place the card over the picture you want. Trace around the card, and then cut out the picture.

3. Use spray adhesive to attach the picture to the back of the card.

4. Repeat steps 2 and 3 until you've made nine playing cards.

To Make the House:

5. Lean two cards together to make a tall two-sided triangle. Be sure the images you picked are facing outward. Hot glue the edges together.

6. Glue a playing card, face-up, to the bottom of the cards.

7. Repeat steps 5 and 6 until you have three triangles.

8. Place two triangles next to each other, and glue the touching edges together.

9. Carefully place the third triangle so it rests across the tops of the two triangles. Glue into place.

NOW TRY THIS!

Make your "house" a home by placing collectable miniatures or other action figures inside each triangle.

WITHOUT A
TRACE

No drawing skills? No problem. This unique
paper lantern project helps you put your
favorite scenes in the spotlight.

What You'll Need:

scissors
8 ½-by-11-inch
   (21.6-by-28 cm)
   cardstock pages
graphic novels
tracing paper

pencil
foam block
thumbtack
hole punch
string of lights
clear tape

Steps:

1. Cut the cardstock into fourths the short way. You should end up with four strips that measure 8 ½-by-2 ¾-inches (21.6-by-7 cm).

2. Choose a scene from your novel that you want to trace. It can be a long panel or several smaller panels. Just make sure the traceable parts will fit on your cardstock.

3. Set a piece of plain white paper over your scene. Trace the parts you want on your lantern.

4. Set one piece of cardstock on top of the foam block. Then place the tracing paper with your image on top of it.

5. Use a thumbtack to punch a series of holes following the outline of your tracing. The holes should be about ⅛ inch (0.32 cm) apart. Make sure the tack pokes completely through the tracing paper and cardstock.

6. Roll the cardstock into a wide tube, and tape shut. Use a hole punch near the top to make two holes on either side of the tube. Then make a cut between the edge of the tube and the hole.

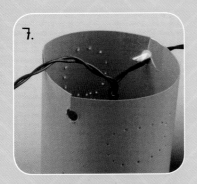

7. Center the tube over a light. Use the cuts in the paper to slip the tube onto the light's string. Then tape the cuts closed.

8. Repeat steps 1–7 until you have enough tubes to cover each light.

SEEING STARS

Leave it to a ninja to find a super-cool new use for a fidget spinner! Transform this nifty gadget into a ninja's star with just a few pieces of felt and some imagination. (Just don't throw it at anyone!)

What You'll Need:

fabric marker or
    permanent marker
fidget spinner
thin cardboard, such as
    a cereal box
compass with pencil
scissors
colored felt
silver or metallic glitter
fabric spray (optional)
glue

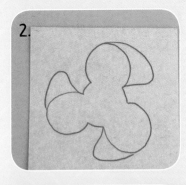

Steps:

1. Use the marker to trace the outline of your fidget spinner onto a piece of thin cardboard. Set the fidget spinner aside.

2. Draw a curved point onto each of the drawn spinner ends. Each claw should angle the same way.

3. Place the metal part of the compass in the center of the fidget spinner. Open up the compass so the pencil sits just outside the border of the center circle.

4. Keeping the pencil and compass at that same width, move the compass over to the cardboard. Place the metal point in the center of your traced fidget spinner. Draw a circle and cut it out.

5. Cut out the full spinner shape, including the points, to make a template.

6. Trace the template onto a piece of felt. Cut out the felt. Then cut out the inner circles. Repeat this step with another piece of felt.

7. To add some flair to your throwing stars, have an adult spray each with a coat of glitter fabric spray. Let the paint dry.

8. Glue fidget spinner onto one of the felt pieces. Make sure the center holes line up properly.

9. Set a felt throwing star on top, and glue into place. Press down to secure. Let dry.

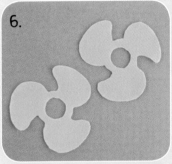

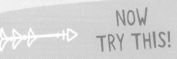

NOW TRY THIS!

Test out different points and edges for your stars. Give each one its own look!

MO'MOCHI, PLEASE

From rice balls to ramen, Japanese food often plays a starring role in graphic novels—and this PB&J-inspired mochi is no exception. These sweet-and-sticky treats are ready to pop right off the page . . . and into your belly!

What You'll Need:

spoon
1 cup (240 mL)
    glutinous rice
    flour (also called
    Mochiko flour)
¼ cup (60 mL) sugar
microwave-safe mixing
    bowl
½ cup (120 mL) water
½ cup coconut milk

food coloring
plastic wrap
oven mitts
powdered sugar
parchment paper
small ice cream scoop
latex gloves
peanut butter
jelly

Steps:

1. Mix the rice flour and sugar together.

2. Add the water, coconut milk, and a few drops of food coloring. Mix all ingredients together until smooth.

3. Cover the bowl tightly with plastic wrap. Microwave on high for two minutes. Stir the mixture. Then microwave for another two minutes.

4. Let the bowl cool for several minutes. Have an adult use oven mitts to remove the bowl from the microwave.

TURN THE PAGE

6.

5. Sprinkle powdered sugar evenly over a sheet of parchment paper.

6. Use the ice cream scoop to drop a dollop of mochi mixture onto the parchment paper. It's hot! Try not to touch it with your hands.

7. Sprinkle a bit of powdered sugar over the ball to help cool it off.

7.

8. Put on a pair of latex gloves. Rub your gloved hands in powdered sugar. This will help protect your hands from the heat and from the sticky rice mixture.

9. Roll the ball around in your gloved hands for a few moments. Then flatten the ball into a disk shape on the parchment paper.

10. Use a spoon to place a small amount of peanut butter in the center of the disk.

9.

11. Add a small spoonful of jelly on top of the peanut butter.

NOW TRY THIS!

Mochi's pretty cool! Use the scoop to make small balls of ice cream. Then pop the ice cream in the freezer until the mochi is ready. Follow steps 5 through 8 to prepare the mochi. Then place an ice cream ball onto the mochi disk. Continue with steps 11 and 12 to seal the mochi. Freeze until you're ready to serve!

10.

11.

13.

12. Fold the edges of the disk together in the middle to form a ball. Then pinch them closed.

13. Gently roll the ball in your gloved hands to seal the edges shut.

13.

14. Follow steps 5 through 13 to make more mochi balls until you have no mixture left. Let the balls cool completely before eating.

NOW TRY THIS!

Not only does mochi make a to-die-for dessert, but it also makes the perfect ice-cream or froyo topping. Follow steps 1 through 4. Then use a spatula or spoon to transfer the whole mixture onto the parchment paper. Cut into small chunks, and sprinkle over your scoops.

TOPSY TURVY

Tops are a traditional Japanese toy. Some simply spin for fun. Others battle it out to see which top can last the longest, knocking opponents out of the ring. Let this one loose with a quick spin of the wrist!

If your top doesn't spin well, try trimming the skewer so it's shorter. It might also help to cut the pointed end a little. If the skewer is too pointy, there won't be enough friction to help your top spin.

What You'll Need:

scissors
manga pages
ruler
white glue

heavy-duty wooden
  skewer or
  toothpick
scrapbook paper
  (optional)

Steps:

1. Trim the manga pages into long strips ½-inch (1.3-cm)-wide.

2. Spread a small amount of glue around the toothpick, near the pointed end. Then wrap a strip of paper around the glued part of the pick.

3. Continue wrapping, pulling the paper tight every few wraps and adding a little more glue. Keep adding strips of paper until the top is as wide as you want it. Gently wipe away any glue that gets pressed out.

4. If you want your top to be a solid color along the outside, cut a strip of scrapbook paper ½-inch-wide. It should be long enough to wrap around the paper layers. Glue the scrapbook paper over the last layer of the paper top.

5. You can shape your top while the glue is still wet. Firmly press up or down on the paper to fan it out into a more domelike shape.

6. Let the glue dry completely before playing with your top.

NOW TRY THIS!

Traditional Japanese tops are spun with string. Wind a length of string firmly around the top of the toothpick about 15 times. Place a finger on the toothpick to hold the top steady. Then pull the string horizontally. With practice, your top will take a spin around the tabletop.

PACK A SNACK

Many students in Japan bring their own meals, called bento, to school. Served in special boxes, they traditionally contain rice, fish or meat, and vegetables. Sometimes the food is decorated to resemble characters from anime or manga! These *Azuma bukuro*-style bento bags will make it easy to wrap up your own lunch.

What You'll Need:

scissors
1/4 yard (111.2-by-23 cm) of fabric; not a
    fat quarter
needle and thread, or sewing machine
sewing pins

Steps:

1. Cut the fabric in half. Then stack the pieces together, with the bright sides facing in.

2. Sew along the long edges. Then flip the tube you made right-side-out.

3. Cut the tube in half diagonally. This will give you two triangles.

4. Fold over the diagonal edges 1/2 inch (1.3 cm), and pin in place. You should do this for all four diagonal edges.

5. Place one triangle inside the other, to make an M shape. The bottom edges should line up, and then diagonal edges should face each other.

6. Sew the diagonal edges that overlap. You'll have to do it for one side of the bag, then flip it over and do it on the other side.

7. Turn the bag inside out. Sew the bottom of the bag shut. Then flip the bag right side out.

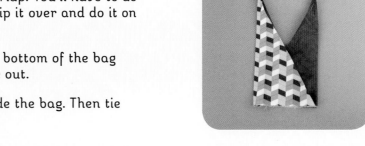

8. To use, place your lunchbox inside the bag. Then tie it shut.

NOW TRY THIS!

A rotary cutter and cutting mat will make cutting the fabric a breeze.

SPECIAL DELIVERY

Stunning Japanese flowers often set the backdrop in manga, so why not recreate some of that floral magic in real life? This Kusudama "book-quet" will bring breathtaking blooms to your bedroom.

What You'll Need:

manga pages   paper clips
ruler   5 buttons
scissors   green stem wire
glue

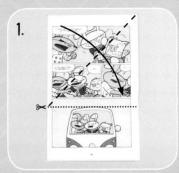

Steps:

1. With an adult's permission, cut 25 pages out of a manga book. Make each page into a square by folding the upper left corner to the right edge. Cut off the excess paper and unfold. You now have a perfect square!

2. Begin with the artwork you want to show on your flower face down. Fold the paper in half, corner to corner.

3. Fold the left point to the top point. Repeat with the right point.

4. Fold the top left flap to the bottom point and unfold. Repeat with the top right flap.

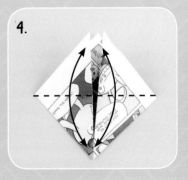

5. Squash fold the left flap by opening it and pushing down on the middle crease to form a kite shape. Repeat with the right flap.

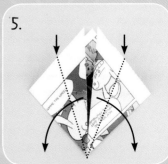

TURN THE PAGE
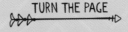

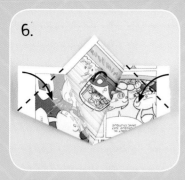

6.

6. Fold the point of the left kite shape. Repeat with the right kite shape.

7. Fold the left kite shape in half. Repeat with the right kite shape.

8. Fold the paper in half lightly to form a petal. Glue the open edges together and use a paper clip to hold them in place until the glue dries.

9. Repeat steps 2 through 8 until you have five complete petals.

10. Glue all five petals together to make a complete flower. Use paper clips or reach your fingers inside to press each set of petals together as you go.

11. Thread the stem wire through the button's back hole. Twist a few times to secure.

12. Insert the bottom part of the stem wire down through the middle of the flower until the button forms the flower's center.

13. Repeat this step with all five flowers, then put inside a colorful vase to enjoy your "book-quet!"

7.

8.

NOW TRY THIS!

For a pop of color, use single-color sheets along with the manga pages. You can alternate petals for multicolored flowers or just put differently colored flowers into your bouquet. Remember the secret to origami success: Every time you make a new fold, be sure to press down firmly and make sharp creases.

9.

10.

11.

12.

CHECK OUT ALL OF THE NEXT CHAPTER CRAFTS SERIES!

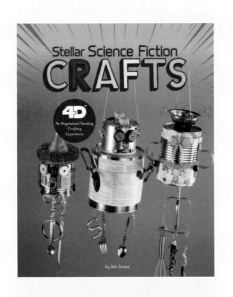

ONLY FROM CAPSTONE!

READ MORE

Montroll, John. *Perfect Pets Origami.* Mineola, N.Y.: Dover Publications, 2017.

Schneider, Christa. *Make It Yourself! Comics and Graphic Novels.* Minneapolis: ABDO Publishing, 2017.

MAKERSPACE TIPS

Download tips and tricks for using this book and others in a library makerspace.

Visit www.capstonepub.com/dabblelabresources

INTERNET SITES

Use FactHound to find Internet sites related to this book.

Visit www.facthound.com

Just type in 9781543506884 and go.